People at Work:
Power Plays,
Mind Games, &
Workplace Bullies

MIN LIU

MIN LIU

CONTENTS

1 INTRODUCTION

Welcome to **People Games at Work: Power Plays, Mind Games, and Workplace Bullies!**

This book is a sequel to my book "People Games: The Ten Most Common Power Plays and Mind Games That People Play". While the original People Games was focused on power dynamics and emotional manipulation between people in their <u>personal</u> lives, this sequel is focused on a different, yet just as important arena of life.

An arena of life that touches every one of us, every single business day: the workplace.

After writing "People Games", which became a #1 bestseller in its category on Amazon, I heard clamoring from many readers of the book asking me to write a version of the book specifically focusing on power plays, mind games, and bullying <u>in the workplace</u>, and so here we are.

You probably found this book either because you were a reader of "People Games" and you want to further your knowledge about emotional manipulation or maybe at some point in your career, maybe even recently, you were victimized by mind games, power plays, and workplace bullying in the workplace, and you no longer want to be blind to office politics and power dynamics.

In listening to the stories of my readers, what has become clear to me is that <u>many</u> people struggle with and/or are victimized by workplace dynamics and the people involved. Just know that you are not alone.

In recent studies on workplace bullying, targets who had greater <u>awareness</u> of strategies to deal with workplace bullying were found to be more successful in their struggle with workplace bullying than those who had no knowledge. As such, it is a massive first step that you have found this book so you that you can gain the knowledge you need to play the "game" in your workplace.

While office politics and workplace dynamics are very broad subjects, this book will focus primarily on the most common power plays and mind games perpetrated by workplace bullies.

I promise you that in the short time it will take you to read this book (probably no more than thirty minutes to one hour), you will have a plan to protect yourself from the most common power plays and mind games that people play in the workplace.

Let's get started…

Cheers,
Min Liu
Corporate Attorney & Author

NEXT STEPS:

DOWNLOAD your **SPECIAL BONUS** "*The Definitive Guide to Upward Influence Tactics*" **($49.99 value, infinite value)** at www.artofverbalwar.com/workplacebonus

In the SPECIAL BONUS, you will LEARN:

- *Tactics for getting noticed by upper management*
- *How to become more influential in your workplace*
- *Ways to stand out among the crowd to your bosses and superiors*

SUBSCRIBE to my YouTube channel, The Art of Verbal War, where people learn to EXCEL at verbal skills at www.youtube.com/artofverbalwar

READ MORE about verbal skills, power, persuasion, and influence at my blog at www.artofverbalwar.com/blog

SEND ME A MESSAGE at info@artofverbalwar.com

2 WHAT IS A WORKPLACE BULLY?

First things first.

Let's start with defining what a "workplace bully" is. In this book, we will refer to workplace bullies as a general term describing a coworker who plays mind games and power plays in the workplace, including but not limited to, the ones described in this book.

Generally speaking, workplace bullies are coworkers (either superiors or peers) who are habitually overbearing, harsh or cruel, typically using manipulation, intimidation or harassment to overwhelm, dominate or control others.

Keep in mind the word "habitual" because even the kindest coworker may engage in such activities (usually unknowingly), but they are not a "workplace bully" when the offending behavior is not continuing or habitual.

Simple as that, let's move on.

3 WHEN DOES WORKPLACE BULLYING OCCUR?

In studies, scientists have found that victims of workplace bullying are generally less independent, less extravert, less stable, and more conscientious. Of course, this is a generalization and not all victims have these traits. It does seem, however, that workplace bullying tends to be a crime of opportunity of sorts; **workplace bullies tend to pick on those who make easier targets.**

If any of these traits seem to describe you, know that part of the solution other than the strategies I'm about to teach you, is to become the opposite of these traits to deter potential workplace bullies. How to do so is beyond the scope of this book, but my advice to you is to do whatever you can to cultivate your independence, your self-confidence, and your assertiveness, and that will go a long way towards deterring potential bullies. ***Become a tougher target for workplace bullies, and maybe you will never even have to use the strategies in this book.***

Research has also found that workplace bullying tends to correlate with aspects of work culture. In other words, studies have found that organizations with the following types of traits may be breeding grounds for workplace bullies:

- a high level of competition;

- radical change;

- a climate of insecurity, e.g. threat of redundancy;

- strong 'macho' style of management;

- hierarchical structures;

- low levels of staff participation or consultation;

- excessive work demands; and

- a lack of procedures to tackle bullying and harassment issues.

A note of caution: If the above describes your workplace, it could be inevitable that another workplace is a better fit for you over the longer-term. No matter what you learn in this book and no matter what you do to build your own independence, self-confidence, and assertiveness, you may be much better served to keep your eyes open and your job options as flexible as possible.

(DOWNLOAD your SPECIAL BONUS *"The Definitive Guide to Upward Influence Tactics"* at www.artofverbalwar.com/workplacebonus)

4 THE TEN MOST COMMON MIND GAMES AND POWER PLAYS AT WORK

This chapter lists what, in my experience, and in surveying my close friends and business colleagues, are the ten most common power plays and mind games that people experience (and suffer from) in the workplace.

You will find a description of each of the power plays or mind games and also specific solutions to prevent the mind games, power plays, or workplace bullying from happening in the first place.

(By the way, make sure you DOWNLOAD your **SPECIAL BONUS** *"The Definitive Guide to Upward Influence Tactics"* **at** www.artofverbalwar.com/workplacebonus)

5 GAME #1: GOSSIP/DISINFORMATION

Description: Studies have shown that gossip and disinformation is the most common form of workplace bullying. The most insidious thing about this power game is that your reputation may be damaged by a "character assassin" before you ever know it is happening.

An underhanded bully may spread rumors about you, and these rumors may not even be true. These rumors, true or not, are intended to undermine your reputation and diminish your power in the workplace.

Example: For example, a workplace bully notices that both you and an opposite sex co-worker were out of the office at the same time. The bully says to others behind your back: "Did you notice that X and Y went out together at lunch? And, Y wasn't wearing her wedding ring!"

Solution: A very important aspect to combating gossip/disinformation is to ensure you have built up your own network of sources at work, so that you can be aware that people may be gossiping or spreading disinformation about you. Ideally, your network consists of people who will have your back when you're not present to defend yourself.

In building your network, aim to have strong alliances at all levels of your organization, above, below, and at your level.

Another aspect, which seems obvious but people prove me wrong daily about how obvious it is, is to guard your reputation at work jealously. Keep as much as your personal life separate from your professional life as possible. Of course, it is difficult to build workplace friendships without being open and candid about yourself, but until proven otherwise, every coworker should be treated with skepticism as to their discretion and ability to keep their mouth closed.

Also, this is yet another obvious point that people can't seem to live up to, but in your dealings with other people, make sure you don't give them ammunition to spread rumors, gossip, or disinformation about you.

Once gossip and disinformation is out, then it becomes harder to stop from propagating. At that point, if you can identify the source of the gossip, then you can confront him/her directly but realize that the damage is done. You can also spread counter-information, both through your actions and through your words.

Finally, don't be seen as participating in gossip yourself, or else you can add fuel to the fire. The harsh truth is, you are hypocritical if you participate in such things while complaining about them on the other hand.

(DOWNLOAD your **SPECIAL BONUS** "*The Definitive Guide to Upward Influence Tactics*" at **www.artofverbalwar.com/workplacebonus)**

6 GAME #2: INSULTS /PUTDOWNS/INTIMIDATION/ THREATS

Description: This type of power play is probably just as prevalent in the workplace as gossip and disinformation, which means so prevalent to the point that the two types of power plays constantly fight each other for the top spot.

Unlike gossip and disinformation however, you will be aware that you are being power played with this power play. This particular power play constitutes a broad category of verbal attacks against a person, a person's traits and attributes, a person's work, or a person's status in the workplace.

In some way, this is probably people's most feared power play because it is in your face. However, because it is in your face, it is at least possible to address the power play directly, as opposed to gossip and disinformation.

Example: X asks his direct report Y to perform a task for him. Y completes the task satisfactorily but X deliberately criticizes Y's work as below average even though it is unwarranted. X does this as a way of establishing his dominance over Y and to instill fear via intimidation in his reports.

Solution: Because this category of power play is so broad, there is no one way to defend yourself. Please see the "Confrontation" section of this book for ideas on how to defend yourself from insults, putdowns, intimidation, and threats.

7 GAME #3: MICROMANAGEMENT/ EXCESSIVE MONITORING

Description: The main actor in this power play is the "helicopter boss", i.e. supervisors who exercise a high degree of scrutiny of, control over, and participation in the work of those they manage. The causes for micromanagement are varied, from a supervisor's insecurity to reasons caused by the victim. Whatever the cause, the work environment becomes unbearable for the victim.

Solution: As a start, it is useful to understand why you are being micromanaged, so that you know whether it is you that is causing he/she to micromanage you. Is there a potential performance or trust issue involved? Are you new to the position and going through a learning curve? Or, perhaps your boss is a new manager who has never managed people? Or have they had others who they managed who were poor performers?

Try to understand whether the micromanagement is specific to you or are you not the only one being micromanaged? If you are the only one being micromanaged, then there could be a specific issue between you and your boss that you need to find out about, understand, and correct. If you are not the only one, then you know the issue is with your supervisor only.

The next step is to "get ahead" of your boss. This means anticipating any criticisms, big or small, he/she will have before he/she offers them to you and having responses prepared for those criticisms. The goal of this step is build trust and to "wow" your boss to such an extent that he/she will become comfortable being more hands-off.

Another tip is to give your supervisor frequent updates (almost too frequently) about your activities so as to limit surprises for him/her. He/she may decide to be more hands off once he/she realizes that these updates take too much of his/her time.

You may even consider talking to him/her to set milestones and regular check in meetings, while agreeing that he/she will be more hands off in between check in meetings.

8 GAME #4: CONTROL/MANIPULATION OF INFORMATION

Description: Within a business, there are two types of internal communication, formal and informal.

Formal communication spreads through newsletters, manuals, emails, memos, staff meetings, conferences and official notices.

Informal communication occurs through the grapevine, which is generally word-of-mouth communication.

In the workplace, information is an extremely valuable asset. You must be plugged into the "informal information network" of your company but know that people understand the value of being plugged in and will try to exclude others (including yourself) in order to have a competitive advantage. In fact, some people may exclude you (such as "forgetting" to invite you) from key meetings or withhold crucial information that you need to know in order to do your job.

Solution: Much like gossip and disinformation, the only solution to this game is to ensure you have built up your

14

own network of sources at work, so you can be aware of things going on at work, especially in your realm of responsibility. You need to be proactive with seeking out people in the know, and you have every excuse to do so, since what you are doing is job-related.

9 GAME #5: SOCIAL ISOLATION/CLIQUES

Description: Unfortunately, cliques still form in workplaces just like they did back in high school. If you blocked high school out of your memory, let's refresh your recollection.

"Cliques" are "a small group of people with shared interests who spend time together and exclude others" and a team as "a group of people linked in a common purpose."

Similar to high school cliques, office cliques tend to socialize during and after work. While there is nothing wrong with that, their "exclusivity" often intimidates employees who are not part of the clique.

Keep in mind that you may think it is a good idea to join the predominant clique in your office. The thing to keep in mind though is that it may not be even be prudent to join the predominant clique from a career perspective. If that clique is perceived by management as the "wrong crowd", joining the clique can actually hurt your career. Cliques that demonstrate gossip and bullying behaviors are especially bad for your career.

Solution:

The first step in dealing with cliques is to pay as little attention to them as possible. Know that you don't need to be accepted into any clique, because you don't go to work to make friends. This is not high school anymore!

Then know that dealing with social isolation and cliques is a matter of expanding your circle of connections at work. Challenge yourself to reach out to colleagues you don't see regularly. You may potentially be overlooking an alliance or mentorship opportunity if you don't.

If there are people you would like to get to know better, step out of your comfort zone and make the first move. You will be glad you did!

10 GAME #6: FAIT ACCOMPLI

Description: "Fait accompli" is a power play where decisions are made without your input and/or affirmative steps are taken to block you from giving input or participating in decision processes that may affect you.

Example: Bob goes on an extended vacation and when he gets back, he finds that his office has been moved from a window office to an inner office. He was not told about this before he went on vacation. By the time he gets back to the office from his vacation, he cannot change what has been done.

Solution: As with gossip/disinformation and dealing with cliques, dealing with this power play is also a matter of expanding your circle of connections at work. You need to be in the loop with decisions being considered and made, and this is not possible if you isolate yourself.

11 GAME #7: STRATEGIC AMBIGUITY

Description: The use of ambiguity as a manipulation strategy to get you to do certain things that benefit the power player.

Example: Often you are ordered to perform job duties or certain things in your job by some vague decision that has not been widely communicated to employees. For example, I used to work for a company that had their headquarters in Europe, and so from time to time, people would tell me that "Europe decided X", "Europe said Y" or "Europe wants Z done". Often times, I would later find out that no such decision or order was given. It took me a while to figure out this was a manipulation strategy.

Solution: In order to not be duped by this manipulation strategy, you need to be skeptical and on alert for the things that others tell you. Don't take things at face value and dig into facts when people tell you ambiguities.

In the workplace, this may rub some colleagues the wrong way, but in my opinion, you should take Ronald Reagan's famous dictum *"Trust, but verify"* to heart. This is your career at stake, so do what you have to do to protect yourself.

12 GAME #8: TACTICAL GAMES

Description: Delay tactics or other tactics used to manipulate you in the performance of your job. It could take the form of deliberate not giving you enough time to think things through. There are too many ways you can get manipulated in your job duties by others, so many that it is impossible to list them all out here. The key is to recognize when you are being manipulated by tactical games played by others.

Example: As a corporate lawyer, it is very common that somebody withholds important information from you so you can properly analyze a legal matter. Usually, they withhold important information so that you can approve some course of action that would not otherwise be approved if all the facts were disclosed.

Or, they may come to you at the last second so that you are forced to make a decision on the spot without adequate information to make an informed decision. These are all "tactical games".

Solution: With these games, you are best off being proactive and letting others know your expectations about their behavior. You should decline to do what they want if they do not follow your rules and if this is not possible, you should give them a polite heads up for the next time.

Should this behavior occur frequently, you should just "call them out" each and every time it happens.

13 GAME #9: WORKLOAD ISSUES

Description: Workload issues are a broad category, but can include an unmanageable workload, unreasonable or impossible deadlines, or being ordered to do work beyond one's competence or ability.

Solution: The first step in dealing with workload issues is accepting that there are some things you just won't be able to accomplish. Don't get trapped into internalizing all your obligations and resist any urge to say "Yes" when you know that you cannot take on more work.

The next step is prioritization, i.e. distinguishing between urgent, important, and less important tasks. Do not let the fact that you have less important tasks overwhelm you, as your tasks will need to be completed in the right order.

Whenever you are asked to take something on, make sure you run through two questions: 1. Am I really the best or right person to take this matter on? If not, speak up and have the work reassigned to the right person. 2. If so, then ask is there somebody who I can partner with to take this matter on? Seek out that person for their help.

As always, stay away from being accusatory. Instead, frame your requests to have work taken off your plate by focusing on quality of work and the company's (and your manager's best interests).

14 GAME #10: BLAMING/BLAME SHIFTING

Description: Some workplaces stay away from blaming and focus on improvement of things gone wrong. However, in certain workplaces, a culture of blaming and blame shifting (i.e. people work to prove someone else acted wrongly) exists strongly. The blame game can even be played with false accusations, which is very common in workplaces with a culture of blaming/blameshifting.

Solution: If you are legitimately to blame, don't become defensive when your boss blames you. When it's your turn to speak, start out by saying "here's what I could have done better."

Follow your response with a summary of what happened and how you could have acted differently. That way, instead of disagreeing with your accuser, you are giving a more balanced view of what happened. This is a chance to point out the direct or indirect part that you played in what happened and to gently correct any misinformation that may have reached your boss.

Sometimes you may be blamed for something you didn't do. Don't "take one for the team" and accept blame for something you did not do.

(DOWNLOAD your **SPECIAL BONUS** "*The Definitive Guide to Upward Influence Tactics*" at **www.artofverbalwar.com/workplacebonus)**

15 THE SIX-STEP PLAN TO HANDLE POWER PLAYS, MIND GAMES, AND WORKPLACE BULLYING

In the scientific literature, scientists have given strategies used to combat workplace bullying the name "coping strategies". I hate this term because it implies that victims of workplace bullying are just passive victims who need to "cope" with being bullied.

Remember: You always have a choice to be pro-active and not just "cope" with workplace bullying and power games, and I am going to teach you how.

While all power plays and mind games are different and cannot be dealt with in a uniform manner, here is a general six-step framework to take the bull by the horns:

Step 1: Emotions Management

The first and most important step is to always put on a positive demeanor to show that you are not bothered by the workplace bully's games. Even better, try to put on a face of mild amusement. Always stay calm and do not show that you are hurt or upset. The goal here is to make yourself a "hard target", i.e. A target that the workplace bully cannot get a rise out of and is difficult to bully.

A workplace bully always looks for their victim's reaction. If you show that you're hurt or upset, that will embolden them and make a small fire grow bigger. If you show no reaction, and even some amusement by his/her silly games, you may even get to stop at this step because the workplace bully may seek a different, easier target.

Another part of emotion management is building your self-confidence and assertiveness generally. Remember that workplace bullies generally pick targets that are "easier", so to the extent you build these things and display them for everyone to see, a workplace bully may not consider you as a viable target and pick someone who he/she can more easily pick on.

Step 2: "Reality Check"

In this next step, you need to make sure that a power play or mind game has actually occurred. If so, has it occurred as a one-off or is it ongoing?

If the answer is yes and it has occurred more than once or twice, then move on to Step 3.

If the answer is no and it is not a repeated behavior, then stop here. You don't want to cry wolf or waste your bullets.

Step 3: Document Each Interaction/Incident

Write down what happened and when. With each interaction, you want to keep detailed accounts of the circumstances, exactly what was said, and who, if anyone, heard or saw it. This step is important both for legal purposes and also to ensure that you can confront the bully with facts and not mere accusations.

Step 4: Assess Consequences

In this next step, think through all the ramifications of responding to a power play or mind game.

As I wrote earlier, responding to power plays and mind games in your personal life can already be risky, but responding to power plays and mind games in the workplace is a different beast altogether in that the stakes can be even higher, and if things do not go well, it can result in you losing your job.

First, you want to assess the costs and benefits of confronting your tormentor.

Sometimes, management may support the bully if you fight a workplace bully. But what if they don't? Are you ready to lose your job? What do you gain from "winning"? Are there other alternatives to confronting the bully? What kind of bully do you think the other person is? Are they "mildly committed", someone who only goes after convenient targets, or do you think they are committed and relentless?

Next, think through your workplace culture.

What are the essential rules for conduct? What are the acceptable and unacceptable patterns of behavior, and the inherent beliefs and values? What are the prevailing approaches to communication and social interaction? Are relationships driven by a formal, rigid hierarchy or ad-hoc interactions? Who has the greatest power? Second and third greatest? How much power is held by others in the firm, individually and collectively? How dominant is this workplace culture? Is it in a state of flux? Has it evolved much during the past few years? Are there any major threats facing the company? How are executives responding to these threats? Has upper management ever fired someone for mistreating employees? Is there currently a bully who appears to have the support of upper management? Has anyone complained about the bully? What was the result? Is there any chance the bully will be harshly disciplined or fired in the future? Do top executives display the types of leadership skills required to recognize the problems of workplace bullying and change the company's culture for the better? Yes, I know there are a lot of questions here, but each one of these questions Is relevant to your assessment of whether to confront the bully.

You also need to assess the bully.

A skilled bully is generally a master of deceit. His/her moves are usually difficult to detect, and difficult to anticipate. Try to understand his/her intentions and watch for patterns in their behavior. What are his/her favorite methods of bullying people? This will prevent surprise when/if he/she attacks next.

Finally, assess yourself as well.

Do you have any vulnerabilities that the workplace bully could take advantage of? Are there types of bullying that are most effective against you?

Step 5: Gather Allies

This will take time, but be patient before you take any affirmative steps to address your tormenter. In this step, you will look for support from others within company, such as other coworkers or managers who are not your direct manager (if your manager is the one engaging in the offending behaviors). Ideally, you will develop alliances at all three levels in your organization: above, below and at your own level.

Having said that, it's good not to expect too much from others. Consider yourself lucky if you are able to find even a handful of supporters.

The way to build alliances is to discuss the behavior of a bully with your coworkers. This should be handled very discreetly, without disclosing your concerns (at least initially).

For example, you can do this over lunch, away from your workplace. You can bring up one of the bully's outward attributes, then watch for their reaction. If you get a positive reaction, you can probe a bit about your coworkers' past experiences with the bully, or if they know anything about his/her background. Of course, don't spend all your time on this subject. Through this process over time, you may find some allies in the workplace.

If you are able to gather enough allies, you may be able to implement a strategy that I talk about in the next section that I call the "hybrid" social support strategy.

Step 6: Implement Strategies (Iterative Process)

Once you have taken each of the first five steps, then you are ready to implement some strategies to help combat the workplace bullying.

There are really just five strategies to respond to workplace bullying, power plays, and mind games, all of which will be discussed in the next section.

THE SIX STEP PLAN TO FIGHT WORKPLACE BULLYING

6

1 EMOTIONS MANAGEMENT

Put on a demeanor that shows you are not bothered by the workplace bully. Become a "hard target".

2 REALITY CHECK

Has a power play or mind game actually occurred, and is it continuing?

3 DOCUMENT EACH INTERACTION/INCIDENT

Keep and gather information that may help you down the line.

4 ASSESS CONSEQUENCES

Determine whether it makes sense to actually take affirmative steps to address the workplace bullying. What cost will doing so extract from you?

5 GATHER ALLIES

Step back before you take any further actions and see how much support you can gather for your struggle with the workplace bully.

6 IMPLEMENT STRATEGIES

Implement appropriate strategies from the "five strategies". Adapt them as needed.

16 THE FIVE STRATEGIES FOR POWER PLAYS, MIND GAMES, AND WORKPLACE BULLYING

In the original <u>People Games</u>, I wrote that "calling people out" is the single most effective tactic for responding to power plays and mind games.

However, in the workplace, the stakes are potentially higher and "calling people out" may not always be the best approach. Sometimes, calling people out may be called for, appropriate, and effective, but a more nuanced and gradual approach may be needed when dealing with power plays and mind games in the workplace.

There are really only five ways to respond to workplace bullying, power plays, or mind games in the workplace. Some people call these "coping strategies". As I mentioned previously, I hate this term because I personally hate having a victim's mindset, as you should too.

Know this: You do not ever need to be a passive victim. You always have a choice to be proactive and not just "cope" with workplace bullying and power games.

Without further ado, here are the five general strategies that people use to deal with workplace bullying, power plays, or mind games in the workplace:

1. **Avoiding**:

Avoiding is an obvious strategy. In this strategy, the victim tries to stay away from and makes no effort to respond to or engage the workplace bully.

A study on workplace bullying found that letting time pass (i.e. doing nothing) stopped bullying only 3% of the time, which means it is an obviously ineffective tactic. You may be the lucky 3 out of 100, but the likelihood is that you will not.

The reason for this is because the workplace is finite and therefore, you cannot really avoid the workplace bully like you can even in school or in other arenas of life.

No matter the type of conflict in the workplace, ignoring it and hoping it will go away will usually not help.

2. **Seeking Support**:

With this strategy, a victim seeks out social support and/or advocacy support within the organization.

"Social support" means support from coworkers, managerial staff, or from people outside of work (friends, family, or therapists). And by "support", I mean talking about the workplace bullying that is occurring merely to get things off your chest, so to say. Of course, this tactic doesn't address the workplace bullying directly, but is merely a "coping strategy". It will not make workplace bullying or power games stop.

"Advocacy support", making use of your company's formal HR process for dealing with workplace bullies, if any, or you may talk to someone in management to assist with intervening with the workplace bully . If there is a formal procedure, you should report the offending behavior as early as you can because the workplace bully could be damaging your reputation behind your back.

If your company doesn't have such a process, or if the person to whom you would report is the culprit, then try to find a "champion" elsewhere, hopefully another supervisor or leader in the company who can intervene on your behalf.

Advocacy support can be effective, but studies have found that advocacy support only achieves success only when the workplace environment is supportive. You should also keep in mind that using a third party to intervene with the workplace bully can also make the bullying even more severe under some circumstances.

Under this heading, there is also one "hybrid" strategy which I should mention. This "hybrid" strategy involves forming an alliance with other coworkers to collectively confront the bully which leverages social pressure to force the workplace bully to moderate his/her behavior. Such a strategy is not necessarily easy to execute, but there are some studies that lend credibility to this type of strategy as being effective.

3. **Destructive Coping**:

Destructive copying is the use of "withdrawal behaviors" to cope with the workplace bullying. It could take the form of ignoring work tasks, taking more sick-leave than one would otherwise take, modifying working hours to minimize contact with the workplace bully, and other forms of destructive coping.

Destructive coping can also result in the victim exhibiting bullying behaviors against others, such as taking out his/her frustrations on others.

Obviously, destructive coping will not help, and will harm the victim even more than it already has, so my hope is that you never go this far to cope with workplace bullying. Please ALWAYS take other approaches in dealing with workplace bullying.

4. **Exit**:

With this strategy, the victim gives up and decides to leave the workplace or transferring to another location or department. This may be a strategy that ends the workplace bullying, but it certainly isn't ideal.

The truth is, most of the above strategies other than seeking advocacy support or the hybrid social support strategy I mentioned above have been found to mostly be ineffective in making workplace bullying stop, which leaves us with the final strategy of "confrontation", which is what the rest of this book will discuss.

THE
FIVE
STRATEGIES

AVOIDANCE

#1

SEEKING SUPPORT

#2

DESTRUCTIVE COPING

#3

EXIT

#4

CONFRONTATION

#5

5. **Confrontation**:

The remainder of this book is about taking the bull by the horns, i.e. confronting the bully.

17 THE "CONFRONTATION" STRATEGY

Under the heading of "confrontation", there are really just two methods:

The first method is "negotiation". By "negotiation", I do not mean negotiation in the traditional way this term is understood. Instead, I mean trying to make the bully aware of his or her behavior in the hope that the bully will see that his/her behavior is unacceptable and stop it.

The second method is "standing up", which is going further and warning the bully to stop the offending behavior. This we will cover shortly, but first let's talk about the essentials of confrontation, which is your demeanor when you confront the workplace bully.

Demeanor and Non-Verbal Communications

Now, before we confront your workplace bully, let's talk about a few preliminary matters. In confronting a workplace bully, your demeanor counts for as much as the words you say. The demeanor you want to demonstrate is that you are calm, detached, poised under fire, slightly amused, emotionally well-balanced, non-defensive, and free from self-serving aggression. This would be in contrast to most workplace bullies, who are overconfident and volatile.

I also mention "non-defensive" specifically because when confronting a workplace bully, he/she will try to put you on the defensive and make accusations and ad hominem attacks. You need to resist the urge to defend yourself when this inevitably happens.

Don't debate his or her on the ad hominem attacks, which is what he/she wants you to do. If you get sucked into that, it would just be deflecting the issue at hand, which is THEIR behavior (not YOURS). If this happens, just say nonchalantly "That's not what we're talking about right now" in order to get the discussion on track.

Negotiation

Negotiation is a good first step towards confronting a bully. In this approach, your goal is to confront the workplace bully tactfully. You confront him/her as soon as possible, and you do it as simply and straightforward as possible.

For example, the workplace bully has been spreading gossip about you. You approach him/her and tell him/her what you heard, and then ask him/her to confirm it. In doing so, you should leave the possibility of you being misinformed so as to give the workplace bully an "out".

Here's a possible approach you could use in such a situation: "I'm sure some wires got crossed, but did you tell someone that Jenny and I went to have drinks after work last week?"

If you are a reader of the original People Games, then this approach may seem familiar. Yes, this approach is "calling them out", but with the twist that you must give the bully at out, a way to save face in calling them out.

In this approach you are merely trying to confirm the bullying. If the bully is merely testing your assertiveness, he may learn that you are not an easy target and stop the bullying at this point. Hopefully, this approach will cause the workplace bully to reassess his/her behavior and stop the offending activities.

If not, then you need to go on to "standing up".

Standing Up

In this final phase of confrontation, you are going to fight fire with fire. At this point, you have exhausted every strategy for fighting workplace bullying, and now you need a more aggressive approach to make yourself a hard target.

You will not ever attack the workplace bully offensively or without provocation, but you will take a stronger defensive approach whenever a bullying event occurs from here on out.

Here are some sample responses, but feel free to develop your own using these ideas.

The *formula* to developing more aggressive responses is to develop responses that are (i) demonstrating amusement at the workplace bully or his/her behavior, (ii) somewhat mocking, and/or (iii) throwing and keeping them off balance.

For example, if a workplace bully rants at you, you can fire back with:

"Don't hold back, tell us how you really feel."
"I sense you may be harboring some anger towards me."
"Let's talk about this, when we can talk."
"Let me know when you're ready to calmly discuss this."
"I can see that you're angry, so let's continue this later."
"Let's get together when you've calmed down."
"I see you're angry, but I don't understand why. Start from the beginning."
"You're obviously very angry. Why?"
"Wow that was really angry."
"Isn't there a more professional way to handle this?"
"Don't hold back! Tell us how you really feel."
"I'm sensing that something may be bothering you."

And, here are some ways you can respond to threats:

"Why don't you think it over? Maybe you'll change your mind."
"I hope you don't do that, but I've made my decision."
"Sorry, but I never respond to threats."
"Do what you have to do, and I'll do what I have to do."
"Your monologues are awesome! Now can I get back to work?"
"Nice outburst! Very effective. Do you practice in front of the mirror?"

Now, if a bully ridicules you, try these responses:

"You have a strange sense of humor."
"That's a rather pathetic attempt at humor."
"Next time, could you raise your hand or something so we know when you're kidding?"
"Don't quit your day job."
"I just don't know how I'd survive without your input."
"No sugarcoating there. Thanks for being so blunt!"
"Wow! That's great. Thanks for keeping me humble."

"Are you feeling okay today?"

"What's really bothering you? You can tell me."

"All I can say is that I really love this company."

"I have an announcement to make: I want you all to know that I really love working here."

"I love you. I really do. You're such a challenge for me."

"Did you just get a haircut?" (If he/she asks why you're asking:) "Oh, no reason. It looks good."

Call someone over: "Hey, come here. I want you to hear this." Then turn to the bully: "Okay, go ahead. Say that again so everyone can see what a comedic genius you are."

Do you get the vibe now now? Using the formula above, you can come up with your own responses that go toe-to-toe against the bully as the situation demands.

Always remember: Your calm and relaxed demeanor is the single greatest weapon you have against a workplace bully.

As a final note, your effectiveness will confrontation will improve with time. Don't expect to master confrontation immediately, as it may take up to a year to get proficient at this. Don't feel bad if confronting your workplace bully feels unnatural in the beginning, I promise you will get it in time once you pick up on the right vibe and attitude, which will just take time to get.

18 CONCLUSION

Here we are at the end of **People Games at Work**!

I hope you learned a lot about the mind games and power plays that people play in the workplace. Consider this as your introductory course to office politics and workplace bullying.

There is always more to learn when it comes to this complex subject, but hopefully the strategies I presented will make whatever workplace bullying you are currently dealing with stop, and allow you head off any new threats that you may face.

Workplace bullying can be a real drag, but with the strategies and knowledge you have just learned, I know you will persevere and thrive.

Best wishes to you, my friend.

Min Liu

Now, I know I just said we're at the end, but its not really the end yet...

Special Bonus Announcements

I have a **SPECIAL BONUS** for you since you are so motivated about your career you that decided to buy and read this entire book:

Go to www.artofverbalwar.com/workplacebonus and I will send you a PDF called "***The Definitive Guide to Upward Influence Tactics***" ($49.99 value, potentially infinite value to those who implement it). This special bonus is not available anywhere for purchase currently, so make sure you download it!

In *The Definitive Guide to Upward Influence Tactics*, you will learn:

- *Tactics for getting noticed by upper management*
- *How to become more influential in your workplace*
- *Ways to stand out among the crowd to your bosses and superiors*

NEXT STEPS:

DOWNLOAD your SPECIAL BONUS "*The Definitive Guide to Upward Influence Tactics*" at www.artofverbalwar.com/workplacebonus

To keep in touch, **SUBSCRIBE** to my YouTube channel, The Art of Verbal War, where people learn to EXCEL at verbal skills at www.youtube.com/artofverbalwar

READ MORE about verbal skills, power, persuasion, and influence at my blog at www.artofverbalwar.com/blog

SEND ME A MESSAGE at info@artofverbalwar.com

REVIEW this book on Amazon.com so that others may more easily find this book and make use of its strategies.

ABOUT THE AUTHOR

Min Liu is the author of People Games, the book Verbal Self Defense 101, an introduction to verbal self defense, the book The New Art of Being Right: 38 Ways to Win an Argument, an introduction to the "art of the debate", the online course Verbal Self-Defense for the Socially Intelligent, a course about defending yourself from verbal bullying, attacks, and insults with wit and social intelligence, and the online course Verbal Domination, a course about dominating and winning verbal confrontations.

He's also the author of The King's Mindset: Twenty Mindsets to Transform Ordinary Men into Kings, a success "playbook" for modern men based on the strategies and wisdom of historical kings and world leaders.

Based in San Francisco, CA, his mission is to help people not only improve, but become EXCEPTIONAL at social and verbal skills. Everything he knows about these things, he knows from his many different lives as an instructor at UC Berkeley, a nightclub promoter, a corporate and securities lawyer, and now, an author.

He's passionate about sharing what he has learned from his transformation from a shy, socially awkward kid into someone who has the ability to use verbal and social skills to get and achieve what he wants in life. He believes everybody has the innate ability to make such a transformation by exercising "muscles" that have not been used very much, and by sharpening the skills they already have.

He gets especially aroused these days by basketball, kickboxing, meditation, songwriting, reading books on psychology and inspirational people, people who are value givers, and most of all, constantly breaking out of his comfort zone and helping others break out of theirs. On the other hand, he absolutely cannot stand mediocrity, unoriginal and lazy thinking, and he really can't stand wearing sweaters.

Media, speaking, one-to-one coaching requests, or other inquiries can be sent to info@artofverbalwar.com.

You can read Min's blog at www.artofverbalwar.com/blog and see his YouTube channel, The Art of Verbal War, where people learn to EXCEL at verbal skills at www.youtube.com/artofverbalwar.

****

ALSO BY MIN LIU

THE NEW ART OF BEING RIGHT: 38 WAYS TO WIN AN ARGUMENT IN TODAY'S WORLD

A modernized version of Arthur Schopenhauer's "Art of Being Right", a playbook of strategies and tactics to help you win arguments in today's complicated society
http://amzn.to/1UNAkU5

VOCAL SUPERSTAR: HOW TO DEVELOP A HIGH STATUS VOICE

Learn the ten steps to develop a high status voice that will increase your influence and authority
http://amzn.to/1Ua3kqD

PEOPLE GAMES: THE TEN MOST COMMON POWER PLAYS AND MIND GAMES THAT PEOPLE PLAY

Learn how to defend yourself from mind games and power plays
http://amzn.to/1n5eqyb

VERBAL SELF DEFENSE 101

An introduction to verbal self-defense
http://amzn.to/1LyZVZM

THE KING'S MINDSET

The ambitious man's playbook to life and success
http://amzn.to/1WCk3m8

VERBAL SELF DEFENSE FOR THE SOCIALLY INTELLIGENT

An online course about defending yourself from verbal bullying, attacks, and insults with wit and social intelligence
http://www.artofverbalwar.com/verbalselfdefense

VERBAL DOMINATION

An online course about dominating and winning verbal confrontations

http://www.artofverbalwar.com/verbaldomination

(DOWNLOAD your SPECIAL BONUS at http://www.artofverbalwar.com/workplacebonus)

****

35365090R00033

Made in the USA
Middletown, DE
30 September 2016